LEAVING FINGERPRINTS

Imtiaz Dharker was born in Lahore, Pakistan, grew up a Muslim Calvinist in a Lahori household in Glasgow and eloped with a Hindu Indian to live in Bombay. She now lives between Mumbai, London and Wales.

She is an accomplished artist and documentary film-maker, and has published four collections with Bloodaxe in Britain, all including her own drawings: *Postcards from god* [including *Purdah*] (1997), *I speak for the devil* (2001), *The terrorist at my table* (2006) and *Leaving Fingerprints* (2009). *Purdah* was first published in India by Oxford University Press in 1989, while Penguin India published *Postcards from god* in 1994, *I speak for the devil* in 2003, and *The terrorist at my table* in 2007.

IMTIAZ DHARKER

Leaving Fingerprints

BLOODAXE BOOKS

Poems & drawings copyright © Imtiaz Dharker 2009

ISBN: 978 1 85224 849 9

First published 2009 by
Bloodaxe Books Ltd,
Highgreen,
Tarset,
Northumberland NE48 1RP.

Second impression 2010.

www.bloodaxebooks.com
For further information about Bloodaxe titles
please visit our website or write to
the above address for a catalogue.

Supported by
**ARTS COUNCIL
ENGLAND**

Cover design: Neil Astley & Pamela Robertson-Pearce.

Printed in Great Britain by
Bell & Bain Limited, Glasgow, Scotland.

For my family,
Simon, Ayesha, Iwan, Gareth, Daniel and Jean,
who recognised the fingerprints

ACKNOWLEDGEMENTS

Several poems in this book were first broadcast on the BBC Radio 3 programme *From Fact to Fiction* produced by Sue Roberts, part of a collaboration with Michael Symmons Roberts and the composer John Harle: 'Landscape with poppies', 'Seed-box', 'Digging up the bones', 'Rush', 'The lost word', 'Today they are shooting the teachers'.

'One frame', 'Sprocket' and 'What is in the box' appeared in earlier versions as part of the project 'On the subject of war' for London's Barbican Centre.

'The missing piece', 'How it started', 'Leaving finger-prints', 'Ceremony' appeared as part of a collaboration with Grace Nichols and John Agard for the Hastings Ethnographic Museum.

'Panditji Will Predicts' is a found poem, from an online astrologer's advertisement.

Acknowledgements are due to the following publications in which some of the poems have appeared: *Atlas*, *The Guardian*, *The Literary Review* and *Magma*.

The Poetry Treatment, an initiative of the Poetry Trust working in hospitals, has displayed 'What she said' and 'What she said later' on loo doors across Britain, fulfilling one of the poet's previously unrealised ambitions.

CONTENTS

Give some tree the gift of green again.
Let one bird sing.

FAIZ AHMED FAIZ

The missing piece

The whole world has shrunk
into a puzzle.

Someone is piecing it together.
Someone else is looking over her shoulder,
the maker in a breathing room.

She is building the picture from the outside
in. First the gilded border, then the story
told in one more jigsawed piece,
the intricate teeth locked perfectly
to reveal the glass, the carafe.
Look now, here, the princess lost
in music, the women playing a drum, a lute,
eyes closed, bodies swaying.

She lifts another piece and hesitates
at a space where nothing fits.
Over her hand another hand is joining in, a glove
of sunshine from the other time.
And there they are, for a moment,
the one who made the puzzle,
the one assembling it today,
the ones who are being assembled,
the instruments they are, the ones they play,

all the hands poised above a hole in the world,
joined in puzzlement.

First gift

Don't expect a silver spoon from me.
I would give you this instead.

A coral spoon from Turkey, fished out
of the Marmara sea where mermaids dined
off dolphins' backs, flicking iridescent tails.

A well-used wooden spoon from Russia,
scarred by banging against a table, bean
and barley flying past the infant's crumpled face.

A spoon discovered in Iceland, carved
from horn and frozen in a spoke of frost, lost
when the Queen of the Mountain tried to feed the Beast.

A shell spoon from Macedonia, a dipper from Peru,
from Fiji a ladle made of the magic kava kava root,
known to stir stories out of earth and air.

Each one fed another mouth
and had good daily use.

Of all the riches in the world
I would give you only this,
no silver spoon, but only this,
a simple way to know their lips,

to touch the hands
that handed down
the hand-me-down.

Seal

Because my fingers fit.
Because the impression your
thumb made on a clay seal tells
me the intricacy of your face, we
meet today as if a curtain lifts. You
invite me in to the places where you
have lived, China, Persia, Peru. This
nest of lines illuminates the colour of
your eyes. Loops dip into the mystery
of indigo pools above your collarbone.
Furrows find a way from fingertip to
forehead and write your lines across
my father's fields. My thumb upon
your clay, my spirals and yours
may be mismatched, but when
I touch the evidence that you
have been, I feel my own
warm blood pump into
your long-dead heart.

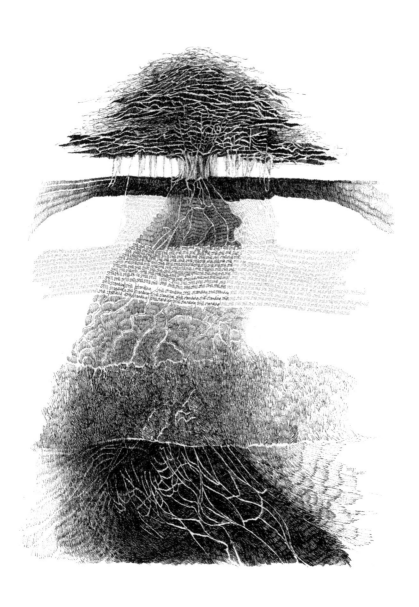

Contract

Is this all it means, the final seal
on a contract?

The business of living no more
than an agreement of skin?

Is the thief no longer a thief
without the hand?

Does the brand on the flank
make you less than you are?

And what of the lover, the leaver
of prints, does this make you mine?

Let us agree to start again
with patience, at the first trace.

In Ancient Babylon, I find an imprint
in clay. In China, a ridged seal.

In Persia, a record of spirals. Loops
in Bologna to rope in a woman or a man.

In Calcutta, on a binding document,
the print of a palm.

Here, the lines race into an untroubled field
and leave it with scratches on its face.

Is that you?
Do you have a hand in this?

Are you stroking the trees
or did you only mean to touch my hair?

Hand of Fatima,
Hand of Miriam

Perhaps this can happen only in a desert,
that two women share one hand.

It could be to do with the austerity of sky, the way
it is stripped down, scraped bare. Then there is
the sound it shares with sand, half wind, half prayer.
Fatima protect me from the evil eye,
Miriam protect us all from harm.

These five fingers have been simplified, pressed flat
into enamelled tin, and in the palm the single eye
opens to let the blue light in.
Prophet's daughter, Moses' sister, I don't see
you fighting over this small light or over me
when you offer me your one shared hand.
Fatima daughter of the Prophet look out for us.
Miriam sister of Moses keep us safe from harm.

I pretend to wear this pendant casually, a trinket
for a tourist, haggled for and bought
in the frantic marketplace. Two for the price
of one, two languages, two guardians
to shield me with a single hand.
Fatima protect me from the evil eye,
Miriam protect us all from harm.

All the travellers end up at one oasis,
out of the airports and the shifting streets.
These things happen in the desert, where sand can stir
and open a single eye of water, where two saviours
between them can muster just one hand,
where tin becomes a talisman.
Fatima or Miriam, Miriam or Fatima
protect us all from harm.

Eye

They stole the whole idea. I was there first.
I was no one's daughter and no one's sister.

They call it the hand of Fatima.
They call it the hand of Miriam.

I was worshipped before those two
were ever born and I was no one's lover.

What I know about evil spells
would make the devil shiver. That hand

is mine, shelter against bad magic and malevolence.
Whenever you see it you will notice the third image

which shifts as time does, changes shape
to be the generous eye, the all-seeing vulva.

Out of my mouth crawled fish and frogs
and the scrawl that they called language

but when I spoke they knew I could be
no one's daughter, no one's sister, no one's lover.

I was the one who ate the sandstorms,
drank the floods and swallowed earthquakes,

the name they lost, goddess, bitch,
the whole world's mother.

Whoever you are

Protect the milk.
Protect the baby who drinks it.
Protect the breast and fill it.
Protect the woman.
Protect the sperm.
Protect the man.
Protect the seed.
Protect the orange trees.

Protect these to begin with.
If you are offering me your hand
I will take it. One of you or two or three,
I will take all the help I can.

Talisman

The street is leering at me strangely, I do not
trust its looks. A headlight nicks my legs as it goes by,
a shadow shifts in the doorway of the supermarket.
In the wrecked public phone box, the phone is dangling

off the hook and something is about to happen.

This is the time when I need protection, something
to keep me safe from harm. I search through the names
on my mobile phone, scroll up and down,
but there is no one I can call upon,

no help at hand and something is about to happen.

I have often felt of late that I should carry a talisman

like the one I saw long ago in the British Museum,
from Rome, 1st Century A.D. A right hand in bronze,
cut off at the wrist, thumb and two fingers raised
in benediction. Up the back of the hand crawled

all the crawling creatures of the earth, a lizard
a worm a frog a turtle a salamander and wrapped over
the curled finger, the crowned snake. I could take
comfort from that now, if I had it here, but I do not

and this is a pity because something is about to happen.

The hand I remember has a ram's head, a baby at
the mother's breast, a table standing on human legs,
and promises sanctuary for all living things, including
me. But I do not have it or anything like it here.
All I can do is step away from the knife of light

and sit in the bus shelter out of the way
because something is about to happen.

CCTV

The footage showed that this was where she came.
She entered the shelter, sat down. Then nothing.
Under the seat they found a discarded table leg,
a worm, a shoe, an ancient stain, a salamander.

Her footprint vanishes

She disappeared without a trace,
they said. If there were footprints
on the sand, the sea got there
before anyone saw and wiped
her off the face of the earth.

If she left a crab crushed
underfoot, if she kicked over
someone's castle, no one
knew, or thought to look for her,
she never got the blame.

She left her fame like a paper flag
you wave for a minute and toss
away. No one remembered.
The wind flapping in deckchairs
never said her name,
and her being there or not
being there was a tide in the bucket
the children played with one afternoon
and forgot to take away.

Not so much as a pebble, not an empty shell.
Picked up by the swell and ground down
in the great mill of the sea

she came back too changed,
grain of sand, grain of star
to do more than fill the vanishing footprint
or cover the ancient scar.

How it started

In Hastings Museum

It must have started with shells
picked up on the beach,
the rumour of a huge world
in your small pink ear.

You reached out across the seas and continents,
brought back the sounds of being born and dying,
eating, drinking, celebrating, praying,
war-drums beating, anklets singing,

all of life like shells, still trailing sand,
collected in your busy hands.
And now you hold them up to let me hear
a whole world roaring in my ear.

Hastings

Hastings
then was just a word. A name
beside a date in my exercise book.
Today the train comes rolling in to this
town, houses marching up a gentle hill.
My pencil strokes were soldiers stock-still
in a poppy field. On the page I drew
a flag on a stick, a warrior protected
by a visor and a shield. I hid his eyes
in shade and Mrs Taylor, marshalling
the jotters, took out her red ball-pen
to mark it with a tick.

I don't know how it happened,
when the battle lines were drawn
with a push and a nudge and a twisted
fact, an arrow in the eye, a rumour a whisper
an unexplained act that dug the certainties out
of the ground, planted them in desks with the
lids slammed down, smuggled them in schoolbags,
carried them home to the place where no eraser
could rub out the wrong and the battles moved
with all of us, red tick, red tick, red tick,
however far we ran.

A place called Battle

We come, not knowing or remembering. We follow
a sun burnt on to an iron shield, an arrow
shot into the eye that might have been blue.
Our Waterloo left far behind, London Bridge, Orpington,
Sevenoaks. Down the compartment a girl is saying,
'No, his eyes are green or greeny grey.'
Tonbridge passes. High Brooms, Tunbridge Wells,
Wadhurst and Stonegate. This is how we find ourselves
in a place called Battle,

a wet field that must have trickled out
of the history book I opened once in Glasgow.
There were dates that looked like footprints then
but now the numbers change to bigger bootprints,
pressed in harder. The boys who made them are present
in this field or another like it. Here it may be green or
greeny grey, there ablaze with poppies
in a place that they call battle.

I can't pretend I've reached here by mistake.
I bought the ticket and chose the destination.
Now I count the rosary of stations.
This has become my weather now. These
conversations are making space for my voice.
Whether his eyes are blue or green or grey, whether
the boys come back from the poppy fields, all this
is my business too. This is where I live with you,
in a place called Battle.

24 frames

A huge set, this field
and the sheep are nothing more
than extras paid for by the shift.
The water expert adds a pond,
the sun is high but the filter's on
and all we need are the boys.

Prosthetics, make-up, hair.
Costumes ready, tunics, shields,
knee protectors, all prepared
and set out with polaroids on hangers
ready for the boys.

Go and round them up from bedrooms
in Sevenoaks, rouse them out of houses
from Orpington to Tooting, call them away
from breakfast tables in Crowhurst.

We are set for battle. The director is here.
The sound is rolling. The camera is on.
We have 24 frames to catch one breath.
Where are the boys?
We are ready for the shooting.

The Game

I know this game, I know how you play it.
You stand in the middle of the world
and shout *Freeze!*

Everything stops dead.
Trucks and buses skid to a halt,
scream and go quiet, the wind drops
into the trees. *Freeze!*

Where there was a stream of people
you see only vertical lines.
If someone was speaking or singing
the words are left hanging in front
of their faces like blinds. One hand half-
way to a handrail, one foot half-lifted
to the step of a stricken train. *Freeze!*

They all know the game.
You make it look easy, if I move I am out.
Just one word.
Into that second you squeeze
all that the world is, all that the time is,
You fix it in a frame to make sure it will never
slide away again. *Freeze!*

You pretend you believe the river is always
the same river and that you can make it
the same river for ever.
Dead still for ever.
Dead. Still.
Freeze! Freeze! Freeze!

One frame

It happened in the time it takes to blink,
just like that. Someone was there

to catch it while it was happening
and put it in a box, easy as trapping a mouse.
It went in, quick, click click khatak!
then sat dead still without a sound.

It sat in its box without the sound
of fire crackling on the burning truck,
the sandbag under the boy's small feet,
the shuffle, the cough, the scraping on brick.

It was captured with skill and a trick of the light,
click click khatak! and that was it,
it never cried out, never put up a fight,
just went and sat in its box without a sound.

It sat in its box without the sound
of running feet or shattering glass,
the message beep on a mobile phone,
the gunshot, the banging heart, the last

prayer. It sat in its box without the sound
of the wind breathing through the grass
or someone whispering, afterwards,
or the questions I keep forgetting to ask.

Blink

I will overcome you, sky.
Face to face eye to eye
I will outstare you.

Are you looking at me?
I said are you looking at me?

Your eye, too huge, is busy
with shifting clouds, jet trails,
light and rising birds and night.

I am still looking at you. You
are still looking at everything

except for me,
except for me.

Sprocket

The frame has slipped out of its sprocket.
Between the drift of waves and the darkroom
the finger must have tripped.

Mottled black and white,
ashes shift in a grate, loose earth
scatters off a spade.

These paper bodies blurred
from being moved too soon.
They have come out to stand
with their backs against a grainy wall.

They make questions that look
like sharp twists of light, but their mouths
make no sound at all.

They have shifted outside the shape
of what they were.

The men in the water appear
to have been shaken out of themselves,
to be followed by their own ghosts.

There must have been a mistake.

What is in the box

Out there is something too big,
too quiet, like a blank page.

An armoured truck is a toy, a convoy
is a line of ants moving towards a distant crack.

The rest is infinite.
This means it will not end.

I am too far away to hear the sound.
It must be there, the breath in the chest,

the click, the blast, cloth
flapping in the wind, tanks rolling past.

I am wondering why they gave me a box
with his wallet, a picture, a badge, an address.

They forgot to put in his voice.

I am wondering how such a small box
can hold such a huge silence.

Landscape with poppies

The sound was the best part,
bubbling through the pipes,
the way breath and water
mix to make happiness.

The old women collected
round the narghile, cackling,
puffing at the reed, till the smoke
patted them on the head.

The haze above them could
belong to poets, but their verses
were the names of neighbours,
someone's daughter, the cadence

of a joke that made
the other women laugh and slap
a thigh or clap a hand
across a malicious mouth.

Sometimes when they were gone
I would put my mouth to the pipe
and imagine being old
and chortling as they did, wickedly.

But the chillum is standing
in the cupboard now
dusty with disuse,
as if in disgrace.

I asked my grandmother
the other day, 'Shall I get out
the narghile? Should I clean the pipes?'
But she shook her head.

'The times have changed,'
she said.

Seed-box

I am lying on my back
in this wide field, the earth
a drum under my heels.
My horizon is poppies
lit up by the sun.

These flowers are wrinkling tissue,
fragile skin on stalks. I am waiting
for the red to drop
across my mouth and eyes.

I am waiting
for the surprise of sky
when petals fall and pods
turn dry, when the wind
comes up and rocks
my cradle of stems.

Then the seeds will jump
and rattle inside their hardened
box,

ready.
Ready or not, here I come.

Digging up the bones

The mud in this country
has a long memory.
It holds bones in its mind
for a century, and is reluctant
to give them up.

It grows fond of its visitors,
treats them as honoured guests,
brings out pistachios, raisins, figs,
conjures up a feast
to make them wish to stay.

These stayed, quite changed from boys
to bones. This is what happens
if people meddle with Pathans.

The mud in this country
has a mind of it's own.

These days guests come uninvited,
and forget to take off their shoes.

Rush

First, destroy the trees. Slash, burn.
Then prepare the ground for seed.
These poppies are like children,
rushing to be born.
These poppies are like girls,
impatient to come to bloom.

Here they are now, ready to be used.
Score the pod, scratch out the sap,
grab at the oozing gum.
This harvest buys bread.

This harvest is a blade, tempered
with acetic anhydride, charcoal,
chloroform.

Clear all the routes and
pathways, it is cutting through
the passes and the gorges,
sped on its way by mules.

The sap called up
from root to pod follows
the rush from the vein
to your god. Find
the grand artery, make
a new road, open the route
for the gush and flood,
the water the oil the saline
the blood,
the string of a lute, a kite,
the flight of a bird.

It is coming straight to you.
Horse Ferry Dust Smack Junk Scag
Black Tar Big Bag Cheese Chip
Antifreeze Ready Rock Train

Dirt Hero Golden Girl White Boy
Dead On Arrival.

Feel it? This rush in the blood.
This bloom in the vein.

The lost word

Think of Freedom as a block
of stone. Chip away
this corner, crack that letter
as if it were a bone.
Hammer it, chisel it
till it's done.

Think of Freedom as a coat
I didn't cut to suit
myself. Snip
this collar, clip
that cuff, chip
this button, chop
that sleeve, hack
the hem, slash
the shoulder, till what
is left is black
hole, less coat
than sack.

Keep the pocket,
tattered as it may be.
It holds the coin
I will have to use to pay
the price.

The price of passing.
The price of wearing
this diminished word.

Today they are shooting the teachers

Today they are shooting the teachers.
Miss Fauzia, Miss Saeed,
yesterday they were here in school.
Miss told me to wipe the board,
then wrote a word
or two, I think 'Geography',
or 'The World'.
I didn't pay
too much attention. Meena told me
what Salma said in the bazaar
and Salma said it was a lie
and then we didn't speak
to each other all day.

Today, getting ready to go to school,
we heard. My mother
said, 'Now they are shooting the teachers.
Tomorrow they will be shooting little girls.'

Meena and Salma met me
on the way to the market. We didn't say
anything about our quarrel yesterday.

Luz Eterna

(after a triptych by Ana Maria Pacheco)

Three frames. Three cuts.
These incidents have been
spliced together. They are not
disconnected events.

Under a reddened sky a city burns.
Barbed wire holds us out or in.
Predators hover above
that tortured body, that broken face,
the screaming crowd.
Hybrid rats with spotlit breasts
gloat over a fall.

This light must be called eternal now.
Give it the sound of whirring wings
and cameras. Record it all,

but look at the way it illuminates
the baby's wondering head.

This is happening in three frames
and in three hundred frames.
Are you watching?
This will go on happening.

Blood coral

The gesture is vulgar but it may do.
You show me, thumb thrust through
the curled first and second finger,
mano fico, the fig hand.
It could do as well as any other hand.

Protect the opening door.
Protect all that has come out of it.
Protect all that will come out of it.
Protect the baby's skull, the blood.
Protect the pumpkin and the bitter gourd.
Protect the water and the food.
Protect the ripened quince, the peach.
Protect the scattered pomegranate seed.
Protect that city. Protect this city,
Protect the ground and the underground.
Protect the boys in the neighbourhood.
Protect the girl at the traffic lights.

Protect all these. Show me what you can do.
If not I will be forced
to look for help from another hand
with more to offer than you.

Spire

Start with mud. Move it,
excavate with any tools you have,
trowel, spade, hands, fingernails.
Then find stone, dynamite it
out of the quarry, hack or chisel
patiently. Pull it all
on carts and creaking wheels,
drag it down dirt tracks and trails
or haul it on trucks
over miles of highway.

Axe on wood, hammer, nails,
the measured thud of taking,
working, making.
This is how, in a minute calculation
of inches and angles, you let the spire
break through to upper air.
This is how you teach stone to lift
its head to the sky.
This is how, out of clumsy earth,
with daily labour, you set free whatever
it is that you call god.

This is how you draw your human breath
in one pure line across an empty page.

Leaving fingerprints

I know this frosted landscape
better than it knows itself, its layers
a busy clock of history, still ticking.

Under my feet I feel the trail of the slug,
the snail, the earth's deep squirm
around an anklet or an amulet, a broken cup.

Lost, the names of the ones
whose fingers made and used
and threw away these things,

written and rewritten in the calligraphy
of roots. The worm's heave
and turn delivers messages up,

scribbled in folds of soil and mud, afterthoughts
that grow to trees, trunks with arms,
branches with fingers, twigs with nails,

scratches on air, tear
after tear on a white page.
These names have given their artefacts away

to be sparse as winter. Here I am, they say.
Here and here for you to see,
fingerprinted on the sky.

Ceremony

Bring me from New Guinea the branch of a tree,
the coconut cup, the snail-silver clod.
Bring me the root and the leaf and the pod
to fashion a birth with the hand of the dead.

I will work on the mask made of Malaga wood,
flesh out its face with fibre and mud,
ease through my hands its breath and its blood
and its half-shaven skull to remember the dead.

Draw over my head the Papuan lime.
Plant in my eyes the promise of fire.
Pull over my face the years of desire,
the greed of the living to honour the dead.

Let his soul pass out of quick clay and bone,
give him safe passage, make way through the crowd
with feasting and dancing and singing aloud.
Let his face live on mine when I laugh for the dead.

Cup

The tree is still holding,
beneath all the layers,
beneath all the writers buried there,
in its secret fingers, a broken
cup

and a cup is a baby, a cup is a womb,
a cup is a skull, a cup makes a room,
a cup is a country more empty than full.
A cup is a heart, a cup is a fall,
a cup is an offering of all you can give.
A cup is an absence, a cup is a lack,
a cup is a boy who came back
in a box because of the promises
we broke

and a broken cup is the silence
when the words are all spilled.

But filled and held up
for me, filled with the moon
for me, the cup is a cup.

The colour of the stories

Write me on foolscap. Write on my skin.
Cover every inch of me with ink, stories
of what you did and what you made,
what you said. This is not a buried history.
The writing will fly off my surfaces.

I have taken the words out of your mouth
and coloured them Klein blue, Istanbul
turquoise, Majorelle purple. They have gone
to another climate, where the sun
gives different colours to their shadows.

They are happy there. When they want to come
home they pick themselves up, stretch
and yawn a little, then with a whoosh!
roll over the cobalt ground and wrap themselves
around my body, blue-black, indigo.

This is how I live. Write me down.

When they walled her in

And when the emperor decided things had gone
too far between his son and the dancing girl
he naturally gave orders that she must be
walled in.

It didn't take the skill of an executioner
or a hangman. All the job needed was a builder,
a man who knew how to slap on mortar
and who had the brawn to heave stone
on to solid stone.

She didn't blame the emperor
because that was a time
when emperors were blameless.
But while the builder was walling her in,
Anarkali lifted her head and began to sing.

The builder didn't think all this
was anything to do with him. He kept his head
down to get the job done, slapping stone on stone.
All it needed was a man like him, who could build
a wall around a song.

She sang about love of course, since that
was the cause of her misfortune,
but she also sang about all the things
in the world that had ever been lost
and she sang about all the things
that were about to be lost.

The builder stopped only once for a meal
of missi roti and onion, then went right on, stone
on stone, building a wall
around a song.

She sang about lost courage, a sleeping man
and words that would never be said to him. She sang
the names of all the people who had gone missing,
the names of their villages and the location
of the wells and all the things that had disappeared

down the wells. The builder thought he heard
his name, but he went on laying stone on stone.

She sang what the cities were before they changed,
the teashops, the hookahs, the poems that lived
there. She sang the names of all the lost
places, Srinagar, Baghdad, Kabul, Gaza.
She sang about losing the gardens. She named
every flower, every tree in the orchard, every fruit.
She named the food that was made in the households,
the ingredients, the spices. She sang about mislaid
letters and languages thrown away. She sang about poets
who would live and die, Faiz, Faraz, Darwish, Shahid Ali.
They all went to live with her behind the wall.

As the last stone was knocked in, the emperor
ordered that the builder should be killed,
as was customary. But he had already died
of a broken heart and Anarkali was singing his heart
with all the other lost and broken things
behind the wall, the wall that he built
around a song.

I would like to say that her voice was always heard
behind the wall, but this would be a lie.
I would like to say that the lost people and cities
and lullabies and all the other missing things
were found again, but this is not the way
it happened.

In the long days and the long nights
the wall was just a wall, no one could tell
that inside there was a song.
People sat in its shadow, leaned bicycles on it,
made phone calls, pissed against it.
They treated it like any other wall.

One day a crack appeared. Another day
a pomegranate blossom burst through.
Someone looked at it and said,
There, that must be a letter from Berlin,
a word from prisoner 46664,
a song from Belfast, a poem from Dublin.

Walling her in

The prisoner had nothing to do with me.
She had been restrained before I arrived,
bound, not gagged.
I hardly looked at her. I was busy
mixing mortar and carting stone.

I started, obviously, at the feet,
doing the job I was given to do,
walling her in, the stones going on
clean and sweet.
Small she might be, but she needed
more space than I would have allowed,
as if she had become a crowd.

It was the scent of her I noticed first
before I came level with her face.
Not fear. Just the scent of a living thing.

I began to lay the stone
in front of her mouth, but her breath on my hands,
her singing so close to my face, did me in.

All the words came and stood
in front of my face, right in front of my face
until I heard her, the woman, I understood
what she was saying. She was saying my name,
the names of my children, the name of my wife,
the name of my village. Singing her heart out.
Singing my heart out.

Singing my heart. Singing.

Anarkali, inside

I am learning to grow with the other creatures,
the snails, the snakes, the slugs, the worms,
my hair a net where ants save stories
and stories save ants, where poets
store the words of songs.

In here, I have started to glow like lapis, amber.
Spiders spin a jewelled skin for me.
They will carry me in all my finery,
carry me to you.

I will not come to you empty-handed
or alone. My eyes will be filled to the brim
with living things, my hands rich
with salamander bangles and lizard rings.

The emperor can only build a palace, he can order
a wall. Will that protect the thing he loves?
Of all that we are making here, nothing is lost.
The earth is keeping us safe
till we take new shapes and live again.

The whole world will sing me
in the bazaar, into babies' ears.
You will hear it again and again,
my name spoken aloud,
Anarkali, Anarkali
in the open marketplace,
in the courtyards and in bedrooms,
in darkened cinemas.

Alive, inside you,
I will be found.

Worm, turning

The crowrasp is coming for me,
beakscrape on stone.
I curl in on myself, smaller,
smaller, shivering. The crow knows nothing.

My body has the glow
of all the things I have rubbed up against.
I have seen such things.
I have seen such things.

On my way through warm earth
I have felt the deep slither of beauty,
the gleam of ore, an ivory handle, copper,
coal in its glory, the remainder of kings,
clean bone, potatoes, her jewelled hand.
The glimmer of my life is worth something
when I have seen such things.

You, the one who stored all these,
not perfect but precious,
fold me in your darkness too,
wrap me in your mercy, hide me one more hour.
I am the witness of the heaven below,
your messenger, your creature.
Save me from that beak, protect me
one more shining night

for I have seen such things,
I have been allowed to see such things.

Squirm

If you want my opinion, though,
that crow should be shot.

Not that I wish for violence or hold a grudge
but it does you no credit. I have worked to be here,
crawled hard and far to be near you, so long
through the tunnel I made in my own image,
scraping at clay to track my own shape.
It started miles down and ended up here
where the light sparkles off eyes
that probe and dart, prod, pry, peer.

I'd wash that crow's mouth out
with earth and soap suds. Listen to its noise,
so greedy, such filth. You can tell where that bird
has been and where it is going. You can tell
even without knowing the language.
Stay away from it.
Can of worms.

What did they leave behind?

They left behind boxes of all kinds, because boxes are always
useful whether they are made of lacquer, enamel, onyx, silver,
sandalwood or pine, to hold a variety of things, an iron key,
a letter, a medallion, a pair of shoes, a lock of hair, a woman.
They left canoes and sailboats, longboats, tall ships, ocean
liners, kayaks, dhows, glittering barges, maps of land and
maps of stars, charts and models of paradise, tablets, scrolls,
winged guardians, gates, instruments for writing, parchment,
slate, plates of clay and copper, honeycombs, golden bees and
scarabs, glass bangles, beads of jade and coral, pearl pins,
amber brooches, silver anklets, pots, pieces of pots, shards,
the perfect amphora from Pompeii, amulet and talisman, rabbit's
foot, wax candles shaped like legs, shrouds, unstitched fabric,
the skin of tigers, the skin of people, war flutes, kettle drums,
trumpets, bugles, bells, horns, whistles, glass baubles to hang
on Christmas trees, tinsel, angels, witchballs, jigsaw puzzles,
saddles, horseshoes, rickshaws, bicycles, Chevrolets, bridges,
steam engines, binoculars, cameras, teapots, trolleys, sofas,
leg-irons, thumb-screws, voodoo dolls, knives, forks, grand
pianos, shell combs, brushes with silver handles and perfume
bottles with the scent all gone, silk scarves, saris of Dacca gauze,
tight flowered dresses, high-heeled shoes with the price still on,
double beds, vinyl, reels of film and screens of all sizes, huge
heroes with bad hair and heroines with breasts like pointy cones,
wall-mounted, cordless and mobile phones, cathedrals, malls,
mine-shafts, tenements and mobile homes, cities built on water,
towns made out of sand, the body of a saint without the toe,
frankincense, myrrh, telescopes to look at stars, tins of sardines,
sewing machines, wax and clay seals, a hand made of tin with
brilliant blue enamelling, stained glass windows, stepped wells,
flyovers, motorways, runways, walkways, escalators, conveyors.
They left behind lists, instructions for how to live and how to die.
They left behind a lullaby written with dew inside a jasmine bud.
They left behind, quite by accident, a love song in a tulip's throat.
They left behind the battered cylinder of a three-tiered tiffin-box.
They left behind a cup still warm from the mouth on the lip.
They left behind a spoon with all of its stories still living in it.

Every working day, Bombay's dabbawallas, tiffin carriers,
deliver hot food made at home by wives, mothers and sisters
to hundreds of thousands of office-workers, using local trains, buses and
    handcarts.
In a city of more than nineteen million people, all the dabbawalla has
to guide him to the owner is a small sign on the tiffin-box.

Only one box in eight million is ever lost.

Dabba's dialogue *or* Tiffin-box talks

No place for words yaar. Alphabet? Phorget! Zara no space
on my lid for commonplace, no good name no home address
no reference number. Tak-tina-tin in VT station off the local
train, allworldover knows me by my fame and my lid sign. I
arrive before wheels squeal on the track only, eleven o'clock
exact! On the spot on the dot tak-tina-tin-tin dabba comes in.

No saala can break this our momentum, dabbawallas dabbas
handcarts running running in formation through chaos phut-a
phut, all clatter and hustle, tiffin-box will reach on the dot on
the spot outside the lift on the exact floor where at tiffin-time
Seema Geronimo Sunil Patil Swaminathanaiyar are expecting
for food hot-hot from the hand of Ma and Mrs home kitchen.

No need for words yaar. No need to speak only when daalroti
raita rice bhindi baingan potato and pickle, home-food comes
dum-a-dum in three tiers of a tiffin. No need for lovenotes ya
this affair is carrying on for hundred years, own home in a tin
with a kiss on the lid delivered by a man who never mastered
abc but reads me like his Mrs' face. Then happiness becomes.

Error

In Bombay time, the dabbawalla must have
arrived at the station with the tiffin-boxes.

I am here in London time, trying to speak
to you by means of an all-seeing
all-knowing box with a keyboard, a printer
and at my fingertips a contact list of hundreds,
all up to date with phone numbers and alternative
addresses. But network diagnostics tell me
I am not connected not connected not

connected.

I discuss this with Rajesh in Bangalore.

My server is down, my site has been removed,
I must have the password wrong. I enter
my name again and again my number my question
my problem my postcode my battery has died
my broadband is gone and the god of the box tells me
sternly that I am unknown access is denied and
I am not connected not connected not

connected.

I have a sharp exchange with Vidya in Bangalore.

The cordless phone has taken a walk and refuses to
come back to be abused. The lights in my hub
are flashing too often or not enough and yes
I have tried switching everything off, changing the
wires and plugging it all back in again. Bear with me
says Seema from Bangalore and then she comes back
fifteen minutes later to say there has been an error I am
not connected not connected not connected not

connected.

In Bombay time it is 6 P.M. and all the dabbas
still know who they are and where they are from.
They have had a day out and about and the mark
on the lid has taken them home.

Meanwhile, my letter-box

makes warning noises. Through its small mouth, the whole outside tumbles in. My name is on everything. I could Snap Up £50 When I Switch to Unlimited Cover with Up to 30% No Claims Discount and No Direct Debit Fee! which no other company can deliver to me. Do I Need a Bit of Sun? I can have it with Worldwide Explorer, Single Trip, Winter Sports and Golf Option! We are Confident We Can Beat And That's a Promise, Promise Peace of Mind and Looking Forward to a Brighter Future You Can Count on Us Call Us Call Us Call Us Now!!! And in case I need more, more names addresses numbers fall out of Yellow Pages. Why do so many people want to tell me some thing? Am I worth it? Is there so much in the world to tell? My letter box screams again. Another army of words marches in, in formation and stands there, shouting at me, shouting, shouting, saying nothing.

Keyboard

With my hands on the dead keyboard I can see the trees
have written on the sky to say that it is midwinter
and I am in a country where they send their leaves away.
Down through all the layers of frozen ground their fingers
are holding on to messages from people who are not my ancestors.
Their mothers were not related to mine. But the messages are still
for me and I am still trying to send a message back to them.

Three ways

Like someone in three minds, dithering
on the hairpin halfway up the hill
in the middle of high-rise cheek-by-jowl
with tumble-down, the road
has muddled along to this point

of indecision.

Three ways, three lights shining in three directions.
One back down past Paradise chemist shop
school and bus stop to where the city and the sea
are tigers roaring at each other in the bay.
One pointing out the pilgrim route
to the secret spring in the sacred tank
that laps at the heart of old Bombay.
One with its finger on its mouth before
the hush of the Hanging Gardens
and the Tower of Silence, the last stop
before the vultures take us all away.

I came cursing traffic, taxis,
handcarts, dabbawallas, buses
that knew exactly where they were going,
swerving round the bend, blowing
hot air and warning horns.
But here, reading the street-signs
under three tube-lights
I begin to count in my blood the names,
each one a choice I may decide to make.

Three ways. Three lights. Teenbatti.
Three lives, all mine to live or leave or take.

My friend the poet says he has become a tree

You have come to the door to wait for me,
an excellent host. But around you the house

has been eaten away by greedy guests,
perhaps you didn't notice, it happened so gradually?

The paint went first, swallowed by the wind
off the Arabian sea, roof tiles thrown up, crumbs

in the beak of a beady-eyed storm, doors devoured
by termites. I had no inkling of this

when I came up the hill from the bay, holding
my memory of you under my arm, a borrowed book

to be returned to polished shelves in a house
that should be full of light and friends sharing food

at a table. Too late for dinner now, and all
the bottles empty. Window frames and lintels

long melted in the mouth of the monsoon,
this house has been feasted on. Word by word,

whole shelves of books have been served up to white ants.
And you are on the threshold,

a few pages fallen at your feet, rooted in the thought
that you will feed the earth,

that you will grow into a tree and that the words
will come back green.

You clutch at brick
but one finger twists up through the ceiling

to a black square above, as if to say, this is where
they were, the words that brought you here. I kept

them carefully between my leaves. And I
am standing with you at the door,

listening,
trying to believe.

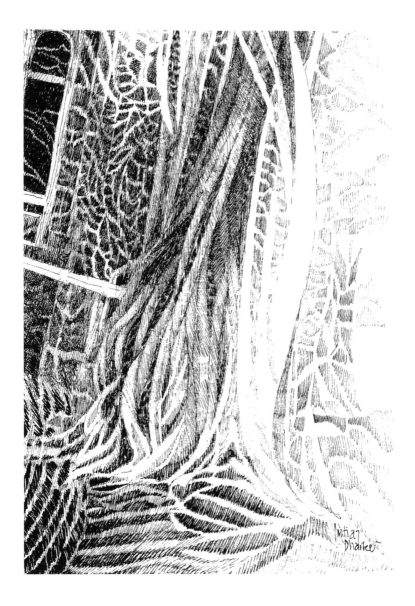

Hand-me-down

Everything here has come
from somewhere else.

That house, built on the edge
of other people's lives, is
made of tin filched from a
building site, blue plastic, wood
picked up from the timber merchants
on Reay Road, hammered together
with rusty reused nails.

That washing line is a piece
of packing string,
the shelf a cardboard box.

That dress has been handed down
from a jaded wardrobe, given to the girl
at the traffic-lights, handed on and on
and mended till it joins the chain
of washing on the line.

The city has been taken and given,
named, renamed, possessed, passed on,
passed through many hands,
my hand-me-down.
One day when I am ready
I too will hand it on.

These lines have been written
and written again in different
times with altered names in other tongues
to repeat the old story in fumbling words.
Just for today I'll call them mine.

Instructions

Before you begin you must
break a coconut.
It lets good fortune in.

Gaddi aa gayi

It happened like this. Their country
slipped out of their hands and broke
like a cup or an earthen pot.
They never spoke as if they remembered
the shape it used to have.

They never cried over spilt blood,
at least not in front of us. It was as if
you reassure a guest, 'Oh don't mind that,
it was only a cheap old cup and anyway
broken china brings good luck.'
And a whole generation swallowed
the nightmares that sounded like trains.
Gaddi aa gayi tation the
Gaddi aa gayi tation the

When the train came in to its destination,
the station drank up the names
of their aunts and uncles,
their neighbourhoods and cities
and our mothers and fathers swallowed
the nightmares that sounded like trains.
Gaddi aa gayi tation the
Gaddi aa gayi tation the

They swallowed the things they remembered
and the cousins who had gone away
with the ghost of the place
that broke with the cup. One day when
my mother was planting potatoes in another
country, she dug up a fragment of china
and looked at it as if she remembered
something that had never been spoken.
Gaddi aa gayi tation the
Gaddi aa gayi tation the

Something she dug out of the nightmares,
something unbroken.
She said the neighbours from the other side
were kind. They took her in and hid her.
They pretended she was one of their own
until they could send her home
Gaddi aa gayi tation the
Gaddi aa gayi tation the

to the country with a different name
to the station on the other side
on another train.

Barkat

If by chance you wake and find on your pillow
jasmine blossoms cold with dew,
you will know that you are loved.

The bud is the knot where everything
begins, someone having gone in the dawn
to gather the flowers for you, the petals
of songs your grandmother sings.
Soja chanda soja
Meri raj dulari soja

You may have nothing
but a large heart and just enough
food on the table for a guest,
but the best of conversations
are garlands in your clever hands,
strung through with poetry.
Tuje nindiya sataye soja
Soja chanda soja

This song is an untied knot.
It will not lie idle
on the pillow or hide in the bed,
but will run out on the street
and when the traffic lights turn
red, stand at your car window
with bare feet, saying
Take this. Take it. I made it for you.

Thumb ring

What her mother said

Here, take this thumb ring too. Even when
your head is covered with the crimson veil,
your eyes hidden and cast down, you can
turn it around to catch in it your husband's
unknown face.

First sight of the man who will
fill your day and night, the face
that will give your children eyes.
Angle it for him alone. This ring
is not a mirror for a crowd.

In it the rest of the world splinters.
The carved room loses all its arches
and its galleries, the uncles and aunts
and cousin-brothers scatter like the dolls
that you will leave behind.

I had a ring like this. I used it that first day
and that first night. Ever since
that is the way I saw your father,
as if in a small mirror, with a twist
of my thumb, his face turned

into a piece of the moon.

Green spiked hair

So I ran away from home with a man
from another country and a small suitcase
that contained a pair of pink suede shoes,
a passport, the condensed sayings of
Chairman Mao wrapped in red underwear
and a copy of *Les Fleurs du Mal* by Baudelaire.

At Heathrow ten years after I had left
I met my father coming off a flight.
Hello? I said. He said Hello, polite as ever,
and walked on. I followed. Excuse me?
I'm your daughter? Ah, he said, not breaking step.
So are you well? And your family?
I'm afraid I need to go now
to catch a connecting flight.

A few years later at another airport
I catch up with him at last.
He has no memory of the incident
when an unknown woman with green spiked
hair accosted him in the transit lounge
claiming to be his little girl

the one he lost
the one who left with a suitcase and
his only copy of the poems of Faiz.

But in the arrival hall the lines come back to him,
Give some tree the gift of green again,
he says, smiling at the words or me,
Let one bird sing.

Road-map

I am driving to Glasgow and I don't
know the highway code. I never had
a driving lesson and was never told
the rules of the road. But this
is the route I fall into, regular
as half past two A.M. I know this lost lane
as well as I know my mother's face
or the veins in the back of my hand.

One hand is on the steering-wheel.
One hand is on my lap. And the third one
is trying to trace the route
on the flyaway road-map.

There's that old man as usual,
walking on the verge, the one who always
turns and stops to look at me, the one
I always ask, 'Is this the way?' He drops
his eyes to my pointing finger and says,
'The map you are using is thirty years old.
The road is long gone.
And did anyone tell you
your mother is dead?'

When you come into my house

says his mother

bring nothing with you.
Come with empty hands.

Cover your head.
In front of the door I will set out
a shallow dish. I will fill it
with the sacred dye. Step into it
and walk across my threshold.
That is when the house will
take in your red footprints
and know that they have come
to stay.

The mark of a wife

according to her friend

You can always tell the good wives
from the bad. See, on this train,
ladies' compartment second class, that one
and that one, they are good, they make
the food fresh for the husband early morning
and every night. The one by the window there
with no bangles, she is no good.

My mother-in-law told me this.
She said, I look for the woman with burn marks
on the wrist. She is the one who will always be
too busy to notice the tava is hot, she will not
feel pain. When the flame is high she will
hurry to turn the chapatti as it roasts, her fingertips
unaware of the heat. Yes, she is the one
who will have the brown marks across the front
of the wrist, across the veins, the badge of honour,
the mark of a wife.

What she said

Never cook your anger with the food.
It will cause indigestion
and disturbance in your house.

Recipe, never written down

My mother never taught me this recipe.
She was a northern woman
and would not cook with coconut.
It's mine. I never wrote it down.

With a machete, slice the top
off a tender coconut.
Drink the sweet water or save it up
for someone you love enough.

Boil rice in the milk of coconut.
Heat oil, add garlic, ginger, a handful of prawn
with tamarind juice, coriander, spice
and one more secret ingredient

that I will have to whisper in your ear.
Come closer. There, did you hear that?
Add it when no one is near,
then stuff the coconut shell

with aromatic layers of prawn and rice.
Seal the top with wheat flour, cook it well.
Keep it in the oven until your guests arrive.
When they break the seal of dough

they will find prawn married surprisingly
to rice in the creamy heart of coconut.
I am telling this to you, no one else.
Make sure the prawn is fresh.

When they ask you for the recipe
always miss out that ingredient.
Pass it on to your daughter.
Never write it down.

Such a perfect bowl of yoghurt

I could complicate this bowl of yoghurt.

I could add mint and cucumber and call it raita.

I could whip it and add salt, black pepper
and water to make lassi.

I could reduce the salt and add sugar
for sweet lassi

or mango pulp for mango lassi.

I could fry mustard seeds in a pot and add
the yoghurt to a cup of gram flour, green chillies
and bay leaves to make a Bombay kadhi.

I could cook it thicker, with more gram flour,
whole red pepper and potato pakoras for a
rich Punjabi curry.

In all these ways I could take this yoghurt
and give it a new identity.

But I want to think about this.
Such a perfect bowl of yoghurt.

Ask the yoghurt what it thinks.
Ask it what it wants to be.

Or just eat it as it is.
Be grateful for its simplicity.

What she said later

I cooked my anger with the food.
They didn't notice. They ate it up
and said it tasted good.

Don't

Don't bring me mangoes or guavas
or figs in your suitcase from Lahore,
she said. Bring me instead
from the giant tree on the magic continent
the plump jamun fruit with the bloom
of longing on the skin.

Be sure to get there before the thieving
parakeets. Under the tree spread out
white sheets. Take a long stick
and tap at a branch to surprise the fruit
out of the tree. It will shower down,
waterfall, fruitfall, on the shock of sheets
that will turn purple with love.

Bring it to me, she said.
The weight and shine of it,
the bite of love's wound.

The bite. Fly with it, take it to her.
Give it a colour, give her
a tongue, she speaks purple, laughs purple,
spits out purple pits.
She abandons words, hung in sharp air
as a parakeet,
keen and there.

Left

It was left on the sheet.
It was left in the snow and the lights on the ground.
It was left at midnight by the dancer's feet.
It was left on the train, the city street,
the muddy lane. It was left by the man
who never complained, the doctor said.
It was left by the rain.
It was left by a lullaby my grandmother sang
and a running girl. It was left
by the boys who never came back.

It was left on a pillowcase and a photo-frame,
on the aisle seat and the handrail
and the page of a book
and a window-pane.

It might be a hint or a clue or a last
attempt at a smile, the ghost
of a leaf or a blot or a stain or the poem
I almost wrote in my sleep

when my lost alphabet found the earth
and planted itself.
It was left, not growing but waiting,
never explained.

Multiple Exposure

Some lie low. Some lie.
Some are devious or play hide and seek.
If the surface is curved you may
have to work with the light
to coax them out.
Build a picture in sections
as you would do with a person,
colour, contrast, brightness
in transparent layers
till something burns through
like a creature that breathes, shifts
shape so it could be a snake
or a dragon or dolphin or mole
or child or woman
lifted simple and whole as a skull

into the light.
When you find it, give it
your attention. It could alter
your view of all that is human

passing like you
passing through
passing through a frame

knowing we may all pass
this way again.

Gone

I see you have been and gone.
Such a small space between
your being here and having
been, just the bedroom door
ajar, and in the kitchen
the kettle and your cup still
warm. You forgot
your umbrella, and now it has begun
to rain. In my mind I see you
turn and look back over your shoulder
towards this room, your
umbrella and me holding on
to it.

The net

Time and wine made a net that pulled you back
to me one night, held you tight
and strong for me.

I tried to hold you, I wove ropes of my hair
and tied your arms to bedposts,
I made a vice of my legs to hold your thighs,
I bound your eyes with kisses, knotted your hair
around the pegs of 'Do you remember?'
things we had done and places we had travelled to.

I kept you for one night. In the
shifting light of next day,
my nets were only dew and you
brushed away my brittle strings.

Love was the gift you hammered through
my palm. I hold it out of sight
with my lifeline
in this closed fist.

Ever since

you left

the glass on my table
the bathroom tap
the handle of my door
have been holding on holding
on holding on as hard
as hard as hard as they can
to your fingerprints.

You left

them so carelessly
on every surface
and now you are out
and about, scattering them wantonly
in taxis and on exit doors and telephones
all over cities all over the world.

Come back.
Leave

if you must. But before you leave,
leave
your fingerprints on my skin.

Cut-out

Take scissors and snap them open.
This is how it starts.
The X on a paper heart,
a kiss, a cut
that takes the world apart.

Take scissors to the scroll, the horoscope.
Cut through the ancient parchment
that has waited years to fix us all.
Here are the pieces of one
and in faded ink, the rumour of another.

Take scissors to the river,
cut the water through its knots
to change its course. Take these abandoned
clothes. Arrange the arms and legs
to make a kiss.

Whatever the predictions told us,
this is how it ends,
the crumpled space in the bed,
the X on the riverbed,

launched on the water, the lost shoe.

Scene

There must have been a body at the scene.
There, where they have made a chalk outline
on the ground, showing how the leg was angled
and the arm stretched out.

There is broken glass and something spilt,
a piece of cloth and more than that.
I can't quite see.

There must have been a crime.
They are dusting the place to lift
the fingerprints. They are turning round
to look at me and whispering.

They are looking at me
as if they can already see
that the prints are mine.

Somewhere else

But I wasn't there, I hear
my own voice say, I couldn't
have been there. I may have no alibi

but at that time I swear I was
elsewhere, admiring the ceiling of the Vatican,
buying a newspaper in a town whose name
I have forgotten, skimming stones over water
at the Loch. I was the one who left
a double kiss hanging in the air. Ask anyone.
I am always somewhere
else.

I wasn't there when they dug
out the nail and found the cross,
the lost piece of earthenware and bone,
the handle of a cup you once used.
I wasn't there when the cranes paused
at the vast and trunkless legs of stone.
I can't remember where I was
but it's a well-known fact, the whole world knows
I am always somewhere
else.

I wasn't there when they celebrated,
lifted their glasses and promised they would
meet again. When the phone rang
and someone answered and afterwards
the instrument was found, still warm.
I can say quite honestly, because
it is always true, that I was definitely somewhere
else.

I was somewhere
else
again.

Somewhere else again

I come out of the station
to a town I have never been in

and as I pass a newspaper stall the man says
'The usual?' and hands me the local newspaper.

I pass a doorway. A child
runs out and hugs my knees.

I go into a café for a cup of tea
and the woman at the counter says,

'I haven't seen you for a while.
Have you been away?'

I say 'I must have been,'
and smile as if I know her

and she says, 'See you again
yesterday.'

Capturing the latent

Take something that changes constantly,
say water. How could you ever hope
to replicate the way it feels?

So too with the fingerprint. Don't
imagine it is fixed. The supple skin
will alter it, the trace of sweat or
lipid, the wet, the push, the slip,
all these can shift the way
the friction ridge meets wall or tabletop.

Technology alone
can never hope to reproduce
the butterfly smudge. Before you grasp
it, it will disappear.

For a true image, a single frame
will not be enough. You must
change the light source, angle and
exposure, build the picture up in many
layers.

This is how you will capture your latent.
But remember this, a fingerprint
must never hope to trap the faint
half-flush that dies along his throat.

I'm sorry to say

there are limits to what it will tell you.
This print

will not say
whether you are a woman or a man,
whether you are black or white,
Caucasian or Asian or African,

whether you can dance or sing
or haul bricks or build a bridge
or play the violin or understand
nuclear physics or paint or write.

All it can say
with any certainty is
that you were here
and touched this thing.

Scene again

No, there was no body at the scene,
just an unmade bed, cold
crumpled sheets, the dip in the pillow
left by a head,
drops of water in the shower. There was
a glass with a tear of red wine,
and something spilt.

They dusted the surfaces, photographed
the prints, matched and overlaid the images,
shot them again in a different light, checked
and checked again.

Then they shook their heads and said
there had been no crime.
I told them I had done it but
they waved me away and I
heard them say
the prints they found
belonged to time.

ID

All it is, you see,
is a hook to hang a person on.

Kinna sona

There is nothing sinister in this.
All we are doing is looking for ways
to make an instant picture of everything
you are. Look at the camera. Roll
your fingertip in this box.

Kinna sona tinu rab ne banaya
Kinna sona tinu rab ne banaya

And you are as god made you, beautiful
And you are as god made you

One day your face turns into paper.
Around the mouth and eyes, across
the forehead, down the cheeks, lines
of words appear, all that you have ever
written, all that you have ever read

Always as god made you, beautiful
Always as god made you

in no particular order, all there,
falling over each other like a crowd.
When you laugh they laugh aloud,
when you open your mouth,
they are the ones who speak.

Kinna sona tinu rab ne banaya
Kinna sona tinu rab ne banaya

And you are as god made you, beautiful

And you are as god made you, unexpected.

Vital signs

All a person is, you see,
is a hook to hang a lifetime on.

The temporary face

I draw your face on the huge sand
in the early morning, when small crabs
run and hide in the holes
I have provided for your eyes.

I go away. Through the day
people come and go, knowing nothing
but themselves, the sun on shoulders,
salt, fish, net. They scuff

your outlines, walk across your mouth,
they put down footprints in your eyes.
This makes you real, peels back
your absence, lets your image heal

like a temporary skin. I learn to
love the thing that has to be erased,
the thing I may not be allowed to keep,
sand that runs away beneath my running feet.

The room with two doors

Pass the wine, we'll leave here soon enough.
We were visitors, we always knew,
even though the host welcomed us,
ushered us in, lit candles for us,
plied us with carafes of wine.

It would be a mistake, however,
to imagine we are free to stay
in this room with two doors,
drinking and eating, telling jokes,
exchanging stories for ever.

The wind swept us in through one door
and is pushing at the other.
Outside, it is waiting for us, running
impatient fingers through the trees,

waiting to take our hearts, browse through them
and toss them to the earth like finished leaves.

Carrying the ashes

I have stopped between
one breath and the next,
one step and the next.

The moth carries its own ashes
when it makes the long journey
round the flame.

When the wine spills out of the cup
the moon comes down to see
its stricken face in the remains.

I have stopped still
in the space between
coming in and going out.

A wing leaves a trace of ash
on my face.

Moth flight to ashes,
blood in the lane,

birds trapped in cages
still sing for the rain.

Lying in wait

Not good enough.
There you are with your gun all cocked,
packed with bullets, the solid weight
on your shoulder and your squinting eye,
awkward, lying in wait for what?

Lying, lying, lying in wait for the prey
that is too quick.

And if you were fast enough, if you were
good enough, if you had perfect timing,
perfect aim, you would be in the game
with your ready gun, you would stand
a chance of bagging the precious thing

that is too quick, that is too quick
for you.

If it was in your sights and you found
the exact moment to pull the trigger
and the light was right, you might
have it at last within your reach, the prize
a bundle of bloody feathers at your feet

brought down and bagged, this bird
of paradise

but it is quick, too quick for you,
too quick

Either way

A sheet of paper. On it I have trapped
a line.
The line could become a wrinkle
a chain of words, a song,
a lace of winter branches,
this line could move in or move on.

In Dharavi the potter decides
the fate of clay. One day it could be
an oil-lamp, the next a lota,
a holder of light,
a holder of water.

The wheel hums round and
the clay has the sound of something
beginning. Thud slap turn
between the hands that shape it
into a pot or plate or urn.
My page rustles uneasily.

The potter and I, with our separate wheels,
hold our own fatelines
in our palms. We could go this way,
we could go that.

Another turn of the wheel
and I might feel, under a potter's hands,
your face turn into light,
my face turn into water.

Panditji Will Predicts

Panditji Will Predicts
Your Future by Palm

for business love marriage studies court case
family disputes such types of all problems.

Who have lost faith in Astrology must meet Panditji.
Mothers & sisters can also meet Panditji.
Industrialists & film actors's have been benefitted by Panditji.

Lucky gemstones also available.
We have famous costly software, with 100% result.

We have DIVINE REMEDIES for
Delayed marriages in females
– In case of woman, due to planetry position in horoscope,
and various curses, marriage is either delayed, some times
it gets very late crossing the marriageable age.
Couple denied of children.
Financial losses in business
Foreign tours
Variety of Curses
Evil eye/unknown suffering/fear

Gem suggestion for gains
Black magic
Health problems
Legal matters/court cases/ divorce

Timing 10 am to 6 pm Fee: Rs.101/-.

Paring your fingernails

This is not hell, but close enough.
In a pista-green room Panditji is cross-legged,
his bare toes twitch, his fingers snap.
The agile assistant snakes high up
to a bulging cupboard, and pulls out
from the very top left hand corner
the map of your life, your personal scroll.

All that you are, all that you were, all
you ever will be, written down more
than a thousand years ago. And Panditji
never asked your name
when you took off your shoes at the door
to come in, just looked at your face
and said, 'Ah yes (in Tamil of course) it's you.'

He unfurls the scroll and begins to tell
your birth your death who you will love
who you will take as a husband or wife
foreign travel health and wealth.
Not one detail spared, it's all
written down, nothing obscured.

Here you may as well lose all hope
of being in control, take your hands
away from your life.
In the face of such knowledge
words get up in your throat
and sit down again. Even the flickering
tubelight stops
to fix you with a sick green stare.

You give up the ghost. Your fingernails
stop growing. Beyond repair.

According to the palm reader

This cross is where the past is buried,
that mound shows your appetites,
from this ridge strong trees will spring
and these creases here are all the children
waiting to be born.

Your thumb shows you will be
difficult, headstrong, stubborn.
You have a strong life line.

*   *   *

That must be the slash through the middle,
like curtains torn apart
or earth split open, when all the prayers
I meant came pouring out
and someone heard,

when lines of fortune, head and heart,
the patterns made by fingertips
broke through what they should have meant,
and wrote out in every language
the letters of your names.

What she asks the palm reader

But which life shows up on my palm?

The one I live, the one I try to live,
the one I live in dreams?

I fall into sleep as if it were cream,
but in that sleep what lives begin,

when the moon is a dinner-plate hung
over a city I have never seen

in a house where I live the dark half of my life.
I get up and walk down the stairs

that swing over the gaping drop where
there should be a hallway

and find the bathroom, a swamp
with green sludge on the floor.

The toilet seat is tin and through the hole
I can see the passing railway track

and when I try to go back, not sure if I should
go back, I can't find the stairs. The doors

I open lead to more empty holes and a wall
that is passing as fast as brick walls passing a

passing train.
So which life can you see? she asks the palm reader.

Which one are you reading now?
The one I am passing?

The one that is passing me?
Which of these lives belongs to me?

What no one could predict

I see that you are busy.

You have been busy all day pulling out weeds
that look like flowers to me, cutting the grass
to make it smell like watermelons, strimming

the edges, stringing up creepers,
strumming the top of the laurel, trimming
the hornbeam hedges so the light dips
over them, a peach about to drop.

I see there is a mist on your arm
and a bloom on the bone at the wrist
when you reach up with scythe and
sheers and secateurs to hack or chop.

If I brought you a fig wrapped up
in a handkerchief of garden, or a tangerine
in a crinkled tissue of sky,
would you stop?

After we have picked the peachy day
and eaten it, if I spread out a window of light
on the grass would you lie on it with me
till we disappear?

Take-away

All kinds of things are moving today
and when they move you hear

the rustle of clothes, the wheels, the squeal
of them taking themselves away.

Somewhere people called
up in rows are shuffling down aisles

when traffic controllers give the sign.
Ready for take-off. A plane

leaves the ground. And in town, at
The Eagle Fish Bar, the takeaway is flying

off the shelves. Fish and chips and kebabs,
pizza delivery bicycles ringing their bells

and something is swinging in the jazz café.
Play it again. Take it away.

Out in the bay
black water is chasing the kisses of light

and fish are flying up the octaves of sea
saying take me away take me away

with you wrap me up with some ships
in the times and take me away

with you, take me today
your take-away.

Someone else

Today the tips slipped off my fingers.

They rolled themselves across a field,
dug down, came back as furrows
in the ground, grew up through trees
and furled themselves into a cloud.
They worked themselves into a frenzy,
a whirlwind, the eye of a storm, a monsoon rain,
then poured themselves back down again to become
a rippled pool, an unwinding spool,
a tangled thread that led to words and messages
passed back and forth between the living and the dead
in a language that had lost its tongue,
a letter a road sign a recipe a poem that brought
the ridges and valleys of other countries back to fall across
the fingertips, still mine, but changed
as if they were glass, as if they were water.

What the palm reader said then

Strange. Your lines have changed as if
they have forgotten where they are going.

I have seen people like these lines.
They stop in the middle of the street. They stand
in the way of all the other people who know
where they are going, the ones who are rushing
to catch the 11.05 from Kandivli to Churchgate,
the ones who are making their way purposefully to Gate 15
because they have checked the clicking departure boards
and the flight has come up *Now Boarding Now Boarding.*

But was it you? Could that have been you I saw
the other day standing in the middle
of the crowd as if you were listening to a river
instead of *This is the last and final call*
last and final last and final

and people walking round you like fatelines
falling away from an open hand?

Last gift

What gift have you brought for me?
I ask the earth, and the earth
replies, the seed of your birth,
this is the gift I have brought for you.

What gift have you in store for me?
I ask the earth
What gift?
The earth needs no words
to answer me, but speaks a tree
and from it sends out leaves, blossom, oranges.
The earth needs no words
to answer me, but sings a stream
that grows to be a choir of five rivers.

What gift have you hidden from me?
I ask the earth
What gift?
The earth needs no words
to answer me, but opens
up what has been kept for me
since the moment of my birth.

My feet stop running,
my hand stops writing,
my heart stops.
A small space opens to accommodate me.
The earth says, my gift is the gift that you
and only you can give back to me.

The mortal coil

I take on the colour and shape of water.
The shadows of your nets are live
in the swell and drift, lifting
against the flare of the sun. You have come
to get me, I see, preparing to pull me in.

In the glare of light above, you have hung
moon faces out to snare me.
You are throwing down these lines,
coiled, uncoiled, woven, broken,
the mesh of what I could become,

the almost welcome, then the sharp recoil
of recognition. The breath breaks free
of its own familiar web
and finds itself still bound too close, too tight,
the absence too fresh,

too quick to flight.

The fish to the fisherman

I am swimming up through the water's
shine and slip to your bright hook.
Look. My body is asking for your light.

Play me, trap me, catch me,
pull me up to you. Lift me
a moment in your hands to admire
my silver, my supple squirm,
my being quick.

Take me home alive. I will die for you.
Make me more than I am.
Divide me.
Feed the multitude.

She was seen

She was seen intermittently
crossing the desert, but does that make her
a woman of the desert? No, all it tells us
is that she was there. It is said that she took on
the skill of appearing and disappearing
in a heat-haze. With her a number of other things
took shape and vanished, things like date palms,
gazelles and giraffes. They sometimes reappeared
as penguins lost in waves of sand.

She was seen in the city, but again that does not
mean she was a woman of the city. She materialised
more like a cat. Around her head swam
a shoal of flying fish but when we examine the footage
recorded by the camera over the bridge we see
something that looks more like a flock of words.
She is walking as if she is stepping through water,
her shoes held high
in one hand.

Breath and shadow

Running water, passing snake. She shakes off
drops of what she has been, takes off the finished skin.

Her river has five names but will not speak them,
knowing the grass is writing them instead.

Her river is not only water, but everything
it lives by, dragonfly, kingfisher, toad.

Her river is more than its own movement,
but everything that runs along with it,

gazelles, girls with green wings on flying feet,
mouths laughing purple from the stolen jamun fruit.

The trees on its banks are a magnet
for beaks, passing parakeets, boys with sticks

who coax the ready mangoes down
and fall on the prize, breaking the perfect skin

with their perfect teeth.
She eats with them.

When she goes to the water to bathe
the blue god is watching, holding his blue breath,

hand poised, waiting to steal her name.
In this river she also lost a shoe.

Reed turns to paddy, banyan to palm,
ridges change to ripples.

She grows away from herself
to lap at other riverbanks and further continents.

Cut the worm and it will grow
a new head, a new tail.

Cut the tongue, it will speak a new language.
Cut the river, it will bleed a country.

Cut the knotted water, it will unfurl a flag.
Call it by another name

when cobble gives way to crane,
warehouse to dock,

the great bridges on a clock of light,
night locked out of the sky by a bolt of gold.

Low grey cloud is mulberry cloth
fraying over the metallic estuary and the angel's wings.

Give it another name and the accent shifts.
The words in her mouth are changing shape

to make a river of voices. No dam, no brake
will hold them back.

What will survive, what will survive of us,
the tar holds her feet, the tar saves her prints,

Yaad na jaye beete dinon ki

and what will survive of us
is love.

How long can fingers hold a river?
It will miss no one, and leaves

with a kiss blown carelessly over a shoulder.
It carries away the warmth of her hands.

Is one river like another?

Like as my fingers to my fingers
and salmons in both, salmons in both.

That river has one name, this one another.

Like as her fingers to your fingers
and stories in both, stories in both.

River runs with the stories, runs deep under ground
where it has found the wall, the builder of the wall,

her bangles, the boxes, the boys,
a mouse, a spark of life, a grain

of a different life down there, where
it remakes itself,

turns to underground train with its rattling doors
and people swinging on straps,

finds brick and earth in the dark,
begins to call itself Circle Line. She misses the sign

for Embankment and decides to stay on, knowing
she will come back to where she started again.

Temple, Bank, the names are flares
that light the dark. The river changes,

changes names.
It has the sound of koels, thrushes,

sparrows. The climate changes in mid-note.
It has the sound that she forgot,

the poem that cut a path through rock,
the explosion that let her through the mountain.

She is on her knees in the aisle, listening.
She came in. She left.

Behind her, everything changed.
She sees in the secret wardrobes of the earth,

folded in crinkled layers, the trousseau
of a happy bride, the unopened faces

of her true ancestors, not bound to her
by blood or cord, not tied by place

or birth. They are the ones who send back word
in the bottom of the broken cup.

Their songs wake her out of sleep,
their words shake her out of the shell.

Their hands rock the cradle till the world
falls out and howls. Buried with all their things,

their trinkets and their amulets,
they unbutton their hearts and open them wide

to show her the complicated truth inside.
She is breathing in there, in the shining layers

of night and snail-shells. She hears all of you
who were here before.

Will you give me yourself? asks one

Your breath and everything you made with your breath.

I give you an onion, another says.

You have passed on *a recipe for water*,
plough down sillion,

shining cobwebs underground, and the sound
of your scratching is the scrawl on the soul.

The world is full of paper.
Write to me.

And you are all writing,
writing to her,

whether you sing the broken hallelujah
or the enormous *yes*.

She is playing this by ear,
making herself up.

The scroll told only half the truth, made her less
than she could be. Ink seeps off its edges,

spills into yours, turns to your river and back to ink.
You are writing her,

writing the secret charm for her,
writing the talisman that will protect her.

Your voices sparkle in the broken water.

She is saying it in my ear, not my name,
but the name of the other world,

the place where we go to disappear
and to find each other, to reach my country, yours,

the thing we share,
the mystery.

Where the river goes

The river has never forgotten its source.
It is not lost
but meandering between unknown banks
its fingers comb the sweet new grass.

What she says now

Unfixed at last, I become
the tumbling stream,
the river that gives
itself away to the sea.

I want nothing.
I own nothing.
The people I love
have only been loaned to me.

What the river says

When I pass you
the sky will turn around to look at you

When I pass you
the apples will fall from the trees into your lap

When I pass you
the water pot will fill itself

When I pass you
the koel will call in other languages

When I pass you
I will bring you the scent of far meadows

When I pass you
buffaloes will find a voice and sing

When I pass you
I will take nothing, not your breath
and not your fingerprints

What the palm reader says now

I do not understand this palm.
It is telling me stories that surely could not
have happened.

Did she travel across the black water and meet
a mythical creature with silver eyes?

Did she scatter the pages of her passport out
of a plane to be carried off in the beak of the wind?

Did she come back quite changed as if her body
had dissolved? Her handwriting turned to sand?

I think I can see two women here, or three. But why,
between them all, do I find a single hand?

I see an eye but its colour shifts like flight
from blue to silver to the colour of water.

I see children and soldiers standing stock-still
looking at each other in the middle of a poppy field.

I see a camera panning over traffic jams and crowded
streets, turning, turning, recording
nothing.

I have never known the lines to lie
but they are telling stories with pictures
I cannot comprehend.

I can no more read this hand
than I can read running water.

What they think she said

Teach me to believe
that nothing lasts,
to wear my life
like a skin of glass
or water that will borrow
my shape and pass